ACCA

Advanced Performance Management (APM)

Pocket Notes

British library cataloguing-in-publication data

A catalogue record for this book is available from the British Library.

Published by:
Kaplan Publishing UK
Unit 2 The Business Centre
Molly Millars Lane
Wokingham
Berkshire
RG41 2QZ

ISBN 978-1-78740-130-3

© Kaplan Financial Limited, 2018

Printed and bound in Great Britain.

Contents

Exam guidance – keys to success in this paper

The aim of this paper is to apply relevant knowledge and skills and to exercise professional judgement in selecting and applying strategic management accounting techniques in different business contexts and to contribute to the evaluation of the performance of an organisation and its strategic and operational development. However it is important to remember that this paper is about application of techniques to real-life situations so you are expected not only to be able to describe and use a technique but to discuss implementation issues and the technique's usefulness in a particular scenario.

APM also has a strong relationship with SBL (Strategic Business Leader) in the areas of strategic planning and control and performance measurement and expects you to have your knowledge in place from PM (Performance Management).

Strategic planning and control

Strategic performance measurement

Impact of risk and uncertainty on organisational performance

Core syllabus areas

Performance evaluation and corporate failure

Performance measurement systems and design

The examination

The format

The examination paper will comprise two sections.

		Marks per question	Number of marks	Syllabus sections examinable
Section A	One compulsory question	50	50	A, C and D
Section B	Two compulsory questions	25	50	One question mainly from E. Other question from any other syllabus area
	Total marks		100	

Total time allowed – 3 hours and 15 minutes.

There will be four professional marks available in Section A.

Candidates will receive a present value table and an annuity table.

The exam will contain a mix of computational and discursive elements.

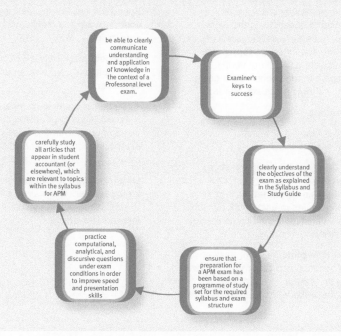

be able to clearly communicate understanding and application of knowledge in the context of a Professonal level exam.

Examiner's keys to success

clearly understand the objectives of the exam as explained in the Syllabus and Study Guide

carefully study all articles that appear in student accountant (or elsewhere), which are relevant to topics within the syllabus for APM

practice computational, analytical, and discursive questions under exam conditions in order to improve speed and presentation skills

ensure that preparation for a APM exam has been based on a programme of study set for the required syllabus and exam structure

There will not always be a unique or correct solution to questions in the APM examination. Alternative solutions will be valid if they are supported by appropriate evidence and workings. Therefore if assumptions are made concerning a given scenario, they should be clearly stated.

Examination tips

Spend the first few minutes of the examination reading the paper.

Divide the time you spend on questions in proportion to the marks on offer. One suggestion **for this examination** is to allocate 1.95 minutes to each mark available, so a 10-mark question should be completed in approximately 19.5 minutes.

Spend some time **planning** your answer. Stick to the question and **tailor your answer** to what you are asked. Pay particular attention to the verbs in the question.

Spend the last five minutes reading through your answers and making any additions or corrections.

If you **get completely stuck** with a question, leave space in your answer book and **return to it later**.

If you do not understand what a question is asking, state your assumptions. Even if you do not answer in precisely the way the examiner hoped, you should be given some credit, if your assumptions are reasonable.

Do everything you can to make things easy for the marker. The marker will find it easier to identify the points you have made if your answers are legible.

Key study tips

Ensure you review prior knowledge from PM.

Revise the course as you work through it and leave sufficient time before the exam for final revision.

Cover the whole syllabus and pay attention to areas where your knowledge is weak.

Practice exam standard questions under timed conditions. Attempt all the different styles of questions you may be asked.

Read the APM articles on the ACCA website and read good newspapers and professional journals.

The examiner expects:

1. assumed knowledge to be in place
2. candidates to use the scenario
3. general business knowledge
4. a rounded view of the whole subject
5. candidates to be able to tackle calculations but the emphasis will not be on these
6. candidates to add value, for example by quantifying comments or discussing commercial implications
7. implications to be considered from a business manager's perspective.

Pass rates are still low. **The examiner recommends:**

1. using the scenario
2. avoiding question spotting
3. good time management – get the paper marked out of 100
4. answering the question asked
5. planning answers
6. that before the exam, students should study the whole syllabus, revise assumed knowledge and practice lots of past exam questions.

Quality and accuracy are of the utmost importance to us so if you spot an error in any of our products, please send an email to mykaplanreporting@kaplan.com with full details, or follow the link to the feedback form in MyKaplan.

Our Quality Co-ordinator will work with our technical team to verify the error and take action to ensure it is corrected in future editions.

Introduction to strategic management accounting

In this chapter

- Planning and control.
- Strategic (corporate) planning.
- Objectives, critical success factors and key performance indicators.
- Long-term and short-term conflicts.
- The changing role of the management accountant.
- Integrated reporting.
- Benchmarking performance.
- Models used in the performance management process.

The emphasis of this section is on understanding the role of performance management in an organisation, to understand strategic management accounting and specific tools. It is important that, in addition to understanding the tools, you can also apply the tools to specific scenarios.

This section also explores the changing role of the management accountant and explores the role of the management accountant in integrated reporting.

Planning and control

Strategic Planning is concerned with:

- where an organisation wants to be (usually expressed in terms of its objectives) and

- how it will get there (strategies)

Control is concerned with monitoring the achievement of objectives and suggesting corrective action.

The performance hierarchy

Characteristics of a mission statement:

Succint Memorable Enduring A guide for employees to work towards the accomplishment of the mission Addressed to a number of stakeholder groups

Strategic and operational planning and control

Strategic planning & control	Operational planning & control
Long-term, considering the whole organisation.	Short-term, based on a set of assets and resources.
Match activities to external environment and identify future requirements.	Rarely involves any major change.
High degree of uncertainty.	Unlikely to involve major elements of uncertainty.
Control by monitoring the strategy and how well objectives are achieved.	Will not lead to changes in strategy.

Strategic (corporate) planning

Strategic analysis

- External analysis to identify opportunities and threats.
- Internal analysis to identify strengths and weaknesses.
- Stakeholder analysis to identify key objectives and to assess power and interest of different groups.
- Gap analysis to identify the difference between desired and expected performance.

Strategic choice

- Strategies are required to 'close the gap'.
- Competitive strategy – for each business unit.
- Directions for growth – which markets/products should be invested in.
- Whether expansion should be achieved by organic growth, acquisition or some form of joint arrangement.

Strategic implementation

- Formulation of detailed plans and budgets.
- Target setting for KPIs.
- Monitoring and control.

Objectives, critical success factors and key performance indicators

An organisation needs to establish SMART objectives and then key factors and processes will be identified that will enable it to achieve its objectives.

Critical success factors (CSFs)	Key performance indicators (KPIs)
The vital areas where things must go right for the business in order for them to achieve their strategic objectives. The organisation will need to have in place the **core competences** that are required to achieve the CSFs.	The achievement of CSFs can be measured by establishing KPIs for each CSF and measuring actual performance against these KPIs. KPIs are essential to strategy since **what gets measured gets done.**

Long-term and Short-term conflicts

Divisional autonomy – individual managers operate their business units as if they were independent businesses – seeking and exploiting local opportunities as they arise

Pressures on managers are for short-term results Strategy is concerned with the long-term

Potential for conflict

Rigid long-term plans can prevent the organisation responding to short-term opportunities or crises

Strict adherence to a strategy can limit creativity and flair

The adoption of corporate strategy requires that the interests of departments, activities and individuals are subordinate to the corporate interests

The changing role of the management accountant

ROLE OF MANAGEMENT ACCOUNTANT

Historically

- Role limted to implementation stage, e.g. responsible for operational budgeting and control.
- Focus is on internal factors and financial information.
- Focus is on the past.

Today

- Strategic role providing information on financial aspects of strategic planning e.g. competitors' costs.
- Uses internal and external information.
- Monitors performance in financial and non-financial terms.
- Focus is on the future.

Burns and Scapens studied how the role of the management accountant has changed in recent years.

Driving forces for change:
- Technology.
- Management structure.
- Competition.

Leading to the following changes

- The role has changed from financial control to business support.
- The new role has been called a hybrid accountant.
- Accountants may no longer work in a separate accounting department.

Leading to the following benefits

- Accountants ensures strategic goals are reflected in performance management.
- Management accountant helps the strategic business unit to get the most from their information system.
- Management accountant can develop a range of performance measures to capture factors that will drive success.

Integrated reporting

The modern management accountant has a role in informing stakeholders of the financial and non-financial impact of the company's decisions.

A new approach to reporting is called integrated reporting. With integrated reporting one report captures the strategic and operational actions of management in its holistic approach to business and stakeholder wellbeing.

The management accountant must produce information that:

- is tailored to the specific situation but remains concise
- is a balance of quantitative and qualitative information. The IS must be able to capture both financial and non-financial measures
- considers how resources should be allocated
- provides an analysis of opportunities and risks that could impact the future
- links past, present and future information. The forward looking nature will require more forecasted information
- considers the regulatory impacts on performance

Benchmarking performance

The objective of benchmarking is to understand and evaluate the current position of a business organisation in relation to best practice and to identify areas and means of performance improvement.

Types of benchmarking

Internal benchmarking

This is where another function or department of the organisation is used as the benchmark.

Competitor benchmarking

Uses a direct competitor in the same industry with the same or similar processes as the benchmark.

Process or activity benchmarking

Focuses on a similar process in another company which is not a direct competitor.

It is important that you are able to evaluate the use of benchmarking in general and each of the types of benchmarking.

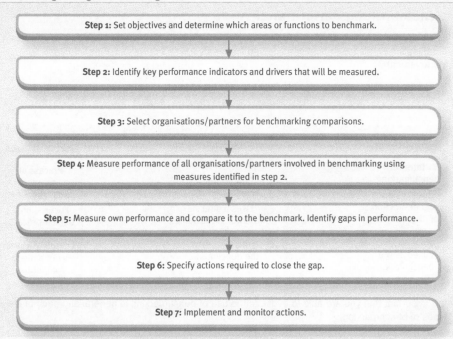

Step 1: Set objectives and determine which areas or functions to benchmark.

Step 2: Identify key performance indicators and drivers that will be measured.

Step 3: Select organisations/partners for benchmarking comparisons.

Step 4: Measure performance of all organisations/partners involved in benchmarking using measures identified in step 2.

Step 5: Measure own performance and compare it to the benchmark. Identify gaps in performance.

Step 6: Specify actions required to close the gap.

Step 7: Implement and monitor actions.

Models used in the performance management process
SWOT analysis (corporate appraisal)

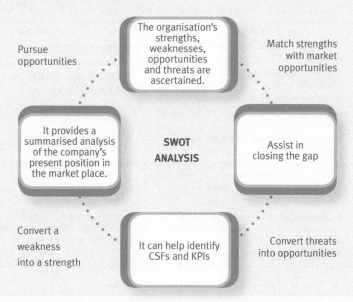

Pursue opportunities

The organisation's strengths, weaknesses, opportunities and threats are ascertained.

Match strengths with market opportunities

It provides a summarised analysis of the company's present position in the market place.

SWOT ANALYSIS

Assist in closing the gap

Convert a weakness into a strength

It can help identify CSFs and KPIs

Convert threats into opportunities

Boston Consulting Group (BCG) matrix

- The matrix shows whether the firm has a balanced portfolio.
- It can be used to assess business performance and performance management issues of an entity.

		Star	**Problem child**
Market growth	**High**	• Is the high reinvestment being spent effectively? • Is market share being gained, held or eroded? • Is customer perception improving? • Are customer CSFs changing as the market grows? • Net cash flow should be measured. • Is the star becoming a cash cow?	**Investment strategy** • Is market share being gained? • Effectiveness of promotional spend. **Divestment strategy** • Monitor contribution to see whether to exit quickly or divest slowly.
		Cash cow	**Dog**
	Low	• Cash generator. Strategy is minimal investment to keep product going. • Is market share being eroded – could the cash cow be moving towards becoming a dog? • Measure net cash flow.	• Monitor contribution to see whether to exit quickly or divest slowly. • Monitor market growth as an increase in the growth rate could justify retaining the product.
		High	Low
		Relative market share	

Porter's generic strategies

An important part of strategic choice is deciding on what basis to compete.

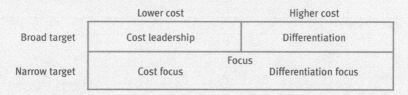

	Lower cost	Higher cost
Broad target	Cost leadership	Differentiation
Narrow target	Focus	
	Cost focus	Differentiation focus

The most appropriate strategy should be chosen to help the organisation achieve competitive advantage and to optimise performance.

Exam focus

Exam sitting	Area examined	Question number	Number of marks
Sept/ Dec 2017	Role of management accountant in IR	1(ii)	6
Mar/ June 2017	KPIs and mission	1(i), (ii)	20
	CSFs and KPIs	4(a)	8
	CSFs	1(ii), (iii)	21
June 2015	BCG	4(c)	10
June 2015	Choice of metrics, SWOT	1(i), (iv)	26
December 2014	Benchmarking	1(iii)	16
June 2014	Mission	1(v)	6
December 2013	KPIs and CSFs	1(i)(iii)(iv)(v)	35
December 2012	Changing role of management accountant	5(a)	12
June 2012	Benchmarking	4	17
June 2012	KPIs	2(a)	12
December 2011	KPIs	2(a)	7
June 2011	BCG	4	20
December 2010	CSFs and KPIs	1 (a)-(c)	20
December 2010	KPIs	4(a)	4

2

Environmental influences

In this chapter

- External analysis.
- Stakeholders.
- Social and ethical issues.
- Political climate.
- Risk and uncertainty.

All organisations will be impacted by the environment in which they operate in and it is imperative that they consider the effect that factors such as risk, the political climate and social/ ethical issues will have on performance.

External analysis

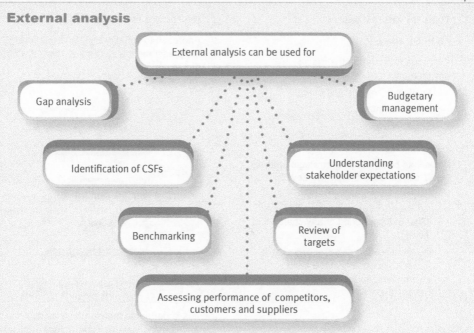

External analysis can be used for

Gap analysis

Budgetary management

Identification of CSFs

Understanding stakeholder expectations

Benchmarking

Review of targets

Assessing performance of competitors, customers and suppliers

Tools for external analysis

(a) PEST analysis

Approach to analysing the macro-environment:

- Political influences and events
- Economic influences
- Social influences
- Technological influences

As well as being used for strategic analysis, PEST can be used to **identify key performance management issues** such as:

- the identification of relevant CSFs and KPIs and monitoring of any changes in these

- the identification and monitoring of risk and uncertainty in the macro environment so that necessary action can be taken.

(b) Porter's five forces

Approach to industry level analysis looking at the pressures that determine how attractive the sector is.

Threat of new entrants

Power of suppliers · · Competitive rivalry · · Power of customers

Threats from substitutes

It is important to measure and monitor the forces using suitable performance indicators.

Stakeholders

Stakeholders are anyone affected by the organisation and its activities. The mission and objectives of an organisation need to be developed with the needs of the stakeholders in mind.

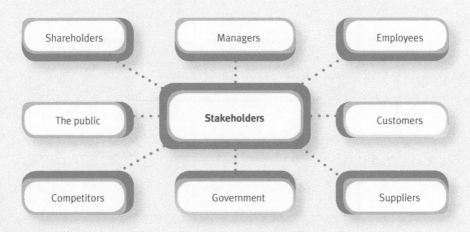

Performance measures should be aligned with stakeholders' needs.

Managing stakeholders – Mendelow's matrix

The interest and power of different stakeholder groups can affect an organisation's performance.

Social and Ethical Issues

ETHICS

- Ethics is a set of moral principles that guide behaviour based on what is 'felt to be right'.

- Ethical behaviour reduces risk and the organisation is likely to be favoured by existing and potential customers, employees, business partners and investors.

CORPORATE SOCIAL RESPONSIBILITY (CSR)

CSR refers to the idea that a company should be sensitive to the needs of all of their stakeholders and not just shareholders. Benefits are customer goodwill, better reputation, happy employees and less chance of legislation being passed.

Political climate

The 'P' in PEST.

Government policy is a key ingredient in the political environment facing enterprises.

- Taxation levels.
- Interest rates.
- Exchange rates.
- Incentive schemes.
- Public expenditure levels.
- Environment protection.
- Restrictive practices.
- Consumer and worker protection.

The impact of fiscal and monetary policy

MACROECONOMIC POLICY
- The management of the economy by the government.
- Aims are full employment, price stability, economic growth and appropriate distribution of income and wealth.
- Influences level of aggregate demand using:

MONETARY POLICY

The government adjusts the money supply, interest rates, exchange rates & availability of credit.

FISCAL POLICY

The government adjusts taxation, public spending and public borrowing.

Supply-side policies

- Views the supply of suitable, cost-effective and adequate materials, services and labour as vital to the economy.
- Largely anti-regulation and anti-government interference.
- Based on the view that regulation prevents the efficient and effective working of the economy.

Green policies/ externalities

- A negative externality is the cost of production experienced by society but not by producers or consumers themselves.
- Growing area of government intervention.
- Examples are carbon taxes, emission targets and penalties.

Risk and uncertainty

Risk is the variability of possible returns. There are a number of possible outcomes and the probability of each outcome is known. All businesses face risk/ uncertainty. Risk management is the process of understanding and managing the risks that an organisation is inevitably subject to.

Uncertainty also means there are a number of possible outcomes. However, the probability of each outcome is not known.

Exogenous variables are variables that do not originate from within the organisation itself and are not controllable by management, e.g. government policy, social factors.

Scenario planning
– looks at a number of different but plausible future situations.

Dealing with risk/uncertainty

Computer simulations
– a modelling technique which shows the effect of more than one variable changing at a time and gives management a view of the likely range of outcomes.

Sensitivity analysis
– takes each uncertain factor in turn, and calculates the change that would be necessary in that factor before the original decision is reversed.

Maximin – involves selecting the alternative that maximises the minimum pay-off achievable. Useful for risk averse (pessimistic) decision makers but can be viewed as overly pessimistic.

Maximax – involves selecting the alternative that maximises the maximum pay-off achievable. Useful for risk seekers (optimists) but can be viewed as overly optimistic.

Minimax regret – is the strategy that minimises the maximum regret.

Expected values (EVs)
– shows the weighted average of all possible outcomes

$EV = \Sigma px$

x = outcome

p = probability of outcome

Useful for a risk-neutral decision maker.
Not useful for one-off decisions or if probabilities are uncertain/ unknown or for a non-risk neutral decision maker.

Shareholders will generally be risk seeking.

Banks are generally risk averse and will want security over their funds.

Impact of risk appetite of stakeholders on performance management

Employees and managers may be risk averse (if, say, job security is important) or risk seeking (if, say, there is a promise of a huge bonus.

Venture capitalists are rational investors who want maximum return for minimal risk but they will be prepared for some investments to fail.

Exam focus

Exam sitting	Area examined	Question number	Number of marks
Sept/ Dec 2017	PEST, risk	4	25
June 2015	Expected values, decision making under uncertainty	1(iii), (iv)	16
December 2014	Stakeholders	1(ii)	14
June 2014	Risk	3(a)(b)	17
December 2013	PEST	1(ii)	11
June 2013	Porter's 5 forces and risk	3(a)(c)	21
December 2011	Risk	1	35
June 2011	Stakeholders	2(c)	6
December 2010	PEST	4(a)	4

3

Approaches to budgets

In this chapter

- Purposes of budgeting.
- Participation in budgeting setting.
- Budgeting methods.
- Variances.

This section of the paper draws on technical knowledge from PM on different approaches to budgeting, but the emphasis of APM is on the importance of budgeting in planning and control and the practical issues relating to the choice of an appropriate method and the impact of budgeting approaches on behaviour.

Questions may be asked on particular methods of budgeting such as zero-based or activity-based budgets. Questions may be numerical and/ or discursive.

Purposes of budgeting

A **budget** is a quantitative plan prepared for a specific time period.

Budgeting serves a number of purposes:

- Planning
- Control
- Communication
- Co-ordination
- Evaluation
- Motivation
- Authorisation
- Delegation

Participation in budget setting

A **top-down** budget is one that is imposed on the budget holder by senior management.

Advantages:

- Avoids budgetary slack
- Avoids dysfunctional behaviour
- Senior Managers retain control
- Can be quicker
- Avoids problem of bad decisions by inexperienced managers

A **bottom-up** budget involves divisonal managers participating in the setting of the budgets.

Advantages:

- Improved motivation
- Increases divisional manager's understanding
- Frees up senior management resources
- Uses local knowledge

Budgeting Methods

Fixed budget – when a budget is prepared for a single level of activity.

Flexible budget – budget prepared with the cost behaviour of all elements known and classified as either fixed or variable. The budget may be flexed to the actual level of activity.

Rolling budget – kept continually up to date by adding another period when the earliest period has expired.

Incremental budget – starts with previous period's budget or actual results and adds or subtracts an incremental amount.

Activity-based budgeting (ABB)

Definition

ABB uses the principles of ABC to estimate the firm's future demand for resources and hence can help the firm to acquire these resources more efficiently.

Steps involved:

1 Estimate the production and sales volumes of individual products or customers.

2 Estimate the demand for organisational activities.

3 Determine the resources that are required to perform organisational activities.

4 Estimate for each resource the quantity that must be supplied to meet demand.

5 Take action to adjust the capacity of resources to match projected supply.

Advantages	Disadvantages
• Draws attention to the costs of 'overhead activities'.	• May require considerable time and effort.
• It provides information for the control of activity costs, by assuming that they are variable, (long-term).	• May not be appropriate for all organisations.
	• May be difficult to assign responsibilities for activities to individual budget holders.
• Emphasises that activity costs may be controllable if volume is controlled.	• In the short-term many overhead costs are not variable.
• Can be useful for TQM since it relates the cost of an activity to the level of service provided.	

Definition

Activity based management (ABM) is the use of ABC information for management purposes to improve operational and strategic decisions.

Zero-based budgeting

Definition

Zero-based budgeting (ZBB) is a method of budgeting that requires each cost element to be specifically justified, as though the activities to which the budget relates were being undertaken for the first time. Without approval, the budget allowance is zero.

The steps

1   Managers specify for their responsibility centres those activities that can be individually evaluated.

2   Describe each of the individual activities in a decision package which should:

  • state the costs and benefits expected

  • be drawn up in such a way that it can be evaluated and ranked

3   Evaluate and rank each decision package, usually using cost/benefit analysis

4   Allocate resources to the various packages.

Advantages	Disadvantages
• Inefficient or obsolete operations can be identified and discontinued.	• Time & cost involved.
• ZBB leads to increased staff involvement at all levels, improving motivation and communication.	• Emphasis on short-term benefits to the detriment of long-term benefits.
• It responds to a change in the business environment.	• Management skills needed.
• Knowledge and understanding of cost-behaviour improved.	• Rankings of packages may be subjective where the benefits are of a qualitative nature.
• Resources should be allocated economically and efficiently.	• Difficult to compare and rank completely different types of activity.
	• The budgeting process may become too rigid.
	• Managers may feel demotivated due to the large amount of time spent on the budgeting process.

Rolling budgets

Definition

A rolling budget is one that is kept continuously up to date by adding another accounting period (for example, a month or quarter) when the earliest accounting period has expired.

Advantages	Disadvantages
• The budgeting process should be more accurate.	• More costly and time consuming.
• Much better information upon which to appraise the performance of management.	• An increase in budgeting work may lead to less control of the actual results.
• The budget will be much more 'relevant' by the end of the traditional budgeting period.	• There is a danger that the budget may become the last budget 'plus or minus a bit'.
• It forces management to take the budgeting process more seriously.	• The budget may be demotivating because the targets are changing regularly.

Variances

Variances are a key element of management control.

1. Targets and standards are set.
2. Actual performance is measured.
3. Actual results compared to flexed standard, using variance analysis.
4. 'Significant' variances investigated and appropriate action taken.

The variances calculated can be divided into planning and operational elements if the original budget was inappropriate.

- The **planning variance** is the difference between the original and the revised budget (uncontrollable by line manager).

- The **operational variance** is the difference between the revised standard and the actual performance (controllable by line manager).

Exam focus

Exam sitting	Area examined	Question number	Number of marks
Sept/Dec 2016	Rolling and incremental budgets	2	25
Sept/Dec 2015	ABC	3(a)	8
Mar/Jun 2016	ABC and ABM	3	25
Sept/Dec 2015	Weakness in budgeting system	2(a)	13
Jun 2014	Variances, budgeting evaluation, beyond budgeting	4	25
Jun 2013	ABC and ABM	2	25
Dec 2012	Budgeting	2	25
Dec 2010	ABC, beyond budgeting	2	25

4

Business structure and performance management

In this chapter

- Performance management in different business structures.
- The needs of modern service industries.
- Business integration.
- Business process re-engineering.

You need to be able to assess and discuss the information and information system requirements of different business structures and discuss the implications of a particular structure for performance management.

An important element of structure is business integration. Performance management can improve by understanding and managing business integration.

Finally, business process re-engineering can, amongst other things, result in a change in structure.

Performance management in different business structures

	Functional organisations (centralised)	Divisional organisations (decentralised)
Information needs	• Performance information required by top of organisation for planning and control. • Data aggregated at the highest level before feedback given.	• Information needs to be available lower down organisation due to the high level of autonomy.
Advantages for performance management	• Better standardisation and control. The IS should aid this communication. • Lower costs since roles are not duplicated. • Defined career path and sense of belonging for specialists.	• Easier to assess divisional/SBU performance. The IS should deliver the correct information to divisional managers, in an appropriate form on a timely basis. • Performance management can be tailored to local needs. • Easier for organisation to grow/ diversify.
Problems for performance management	• Difficult to assess performance of individual products or markets. • Dysfunctional behaviour of managers. • Slow decision making. • Hard to grow/ diversify.	• Cost of duplication of functions. • Transfer pricing issues. • Potential problems with lack of goal congruence.

Network organisation	
Information needs	• The organisation needs to establish shared goals and contractual agreements. • Those responsible for regulating performance will need information for decision making. • Each party needs feedback on its performance. The IS will need to be sophisticated with the ability to gather and process the information from all parties.
Advantages for performance management	• Flexibility to meet project needs. • Can exploit market opportunities. • Can compete with larger organisations. • Lower infrastructure costs.
Disadvantages for performance management	• Difficult to agree common goals and measures. • Planning and control difficult. • Monitoring of the workforce difficult. • Information gathering difficult if IS not compatible. • Loss of competitive advantage if partners work for competitors. Many of the problems can be addressed using a service level agreement (SLA).

Problems associated with complex business structures

Business structure	Problems planning, measuring and controlling performance
Joint venture	• Different partners may have different goals so a variety of performance measures will be required. • Attributing accountability is difficult. • Reporting and sharing information difficult if systems not integrated. • Quality, cost control and risk management difficult if partners have different opinions. • Security of information a concern.
Strategic alliance	Many of the difficulties above apply but more specifically: • Independence retained making it difficult to put common performance measures in place. • Security of confidential information more of a concern due to a lack of separate legal entity.
Multinationals	• Planning, control and co-ordination of subsidiaries can be difficult. • Measuring and reporting performance difficult if common systems don't exist. • Open to greater levels of uncertainty, e.g. due to exchange rate movements.

The needs of modern service industries

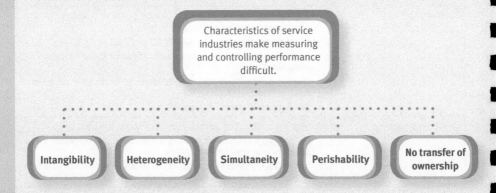

These differences will result in different objectives and CSFs. Appropriate performance measures should be established.

Business integration

Definition

Business integration means that all aspects of the business must be aligned to secure the most efficient use of the organisation's resources so that it can achieve its objectives effectively.

Processes are viewed as complete entities from initial order to final delivery.

Porter's value chain

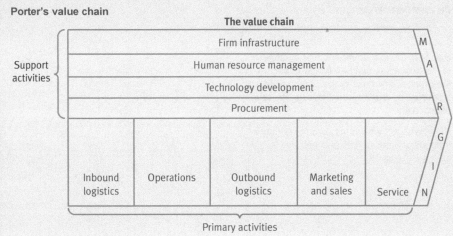

The value chain

The value chain model

- Is based around **activities** rather than functional departments. It shows how each activity adds to competitive advantage.
- Emphasises linkages and critical success factors within activities and for the value chain as a whole.

Mckinsey's 7s model

Mckinsey's 7s model describes an organisation as consisting of seven interrelated internal elements.

Business process re-engineering (BPR)

The way in which an organisation's activities function and inter-relate constitute an organisation's processes.

Business process re-engineering is the fundamental rethinking and radical redesign of business processes to achieve dramatic improvements in critical, contemporary measures of performance, such as cost, quality, service and speed.

The influence of BPR on the organisation:

BPR cuts across traditional departmental lines	• Change to process view will require change in culture with a move to process teams and not functional departments • Employees will need to retrain • Communication and leadership from senior management essential • BPR results in more integration and use of IT
BPR may result in improved organisational performance:	• Looks at how core processes can be honed to achieve corporate goals • Revolves around customer needs, key to competitive advantage • Can help eliminate unnecessary activities • Process should be made cheaper
Practical problems include:	• Perception by staff that BPR is all about cost cutting • Staff may feel devalued or demotivated if role changes • Often strips out middle managers leading to poor control and co-ordination • May utilise outsourcing with potential quality/ flexibility implications • May purely result in automation of processes and not redesign
Changes to performance management system	• Systems redesigned to capture new performance measurement data • Reward system aligned to new measures

Exam sitting	Area examined	Question number	Number of marks
Mar/June 2016	BPR	2	25
June 2015	Value chain	1(v)	6
June 2014	BPR	2(a)(b)	17
June 2014	Complex business structures	3(c)	8
June 2013	Differences between services and manufacturing organisations	1(i)	5
June 2013	Change in divisional structure	4(c)	9
June 2012	Performance management and measurement in complex business structures	5	17
June 2012	Complex business structures	5	17

5

The impact of information technology

In this chapter

- Sources of management information.
- Compatibility of management accounting and management accounting information.
- Developing management accounting systems.
- The need for continual systems development.
- IT developments.
- Big Data.

Exam focus

Managers need access to good information in order to be able to effectively plan, direct and control the activities they are responsible for. It is important to understand the sources of management information and how advances in technology have resulted in the development of effective management accounting systems.

Sources of management information

Information can be obtained from **internal** and **external** sources. Much is free, but some comes at a cost, such as:

- most information from business enquiry agents is charged for
- banks and financial journals often sell surveys and forecasts
- internet databases may charge a subscription
- government statistics, forecasts and reports may be charged for.

Internal sources	External sources
• Sales ledger system	• Suppliers
• Purchase ledger system	• Newspapers and journals
• Payroll system	• Government
• Fixed asset system	• Customers
• Production	• Employees
• Sales and marketing	• Banks
	• Business enquiry agents
	• Internet

Compatibility of management accounting and management accounting information

Management accounting information may be used to:

- assess performance
- value inventories
- make future plans
- control the business
- make decisions.

Management accounting involves the provision and analysis of detailed information to help managers to run the business today and in the future.

The objectives of management accounting should be compatible with management accounting information.

Developing management accounting systems

Definition

A management information system (MIS) converts internal and external data into useful information which is then communicated to managers at all levels and across all functions to enable them to make timely and effective decisions for planning, directing and controlling activities.

There are a number of types of MIS:

Executive information system (EIS)	**Decision support system (DSS)**	**Expert system**
• Gives senior managers access to internal and external information	• Aids managers in making decisions	• Hold specialist knowledge
• Presented in a user-friendly summarised form	• Predicts the consequences of a number of possible scenarios	• Allow non-experts to interrogate for information, advice and recommended decisions
• Option to drill down to a greater level of detail	• Manager then uses their judgement to make the final decision	

The need for continual systems development

Information and accounting systems need to be developed continually otherwise they will become out of date.

- Need for faster innovation
- Shift from manufacturing to service industries
- New manufacturing processes e.g. JIT
- Business growth and diversification
- Availability of new technologies
- Need for continuous improvement of systems
- Increased competition
- New accounting developments

IT developments

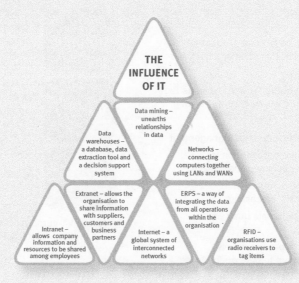

KAPLAN PUBLISHING

Big data

Definition

Extremely large collections of data that may be analysed to reveal patterns, trends and associations.

The processing of Big Data is known as Big Data analytics, for example using Hadoop software.

Big Data and Performance Management

- It can help the organisation to understand customers' needs and preferences.
- It can improve forecasting.
- It can help automate business processes.
- It can help to provide detailed, relevant and up to date performance measurement.

Characterised by the 3Vs

Volume
Organisations now hold huge volumes of data, for example on customer purchases.

Variety
Data can be financial or non-financial, internal or external, structured or unstructured.

Velocity
The data needs to be turned into useful information quickly.

A fourth 'V', **veracity**, is sometimes included, i.e. is the data accurate?'

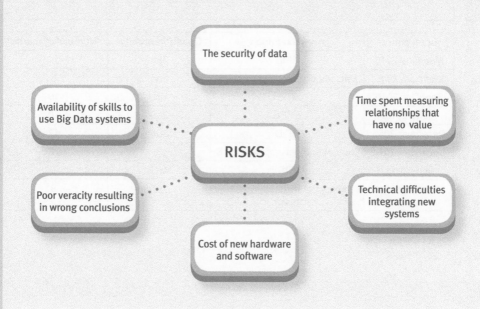

Exam sitting	Area examined	Question number	Number of marks
Mar/June 2016	RFID	2(a)	14
Mar/June 2016	Data warehouse, loyalty cards	1(v)	8
Sept/Dec 2015	ERPS	1(iv)	10
June 2015	ERPS	2(a)	10
December 2013	RFID	3(a)	12
December 2011	Control and development of IS	3	20
June 2011	EIS	1(c)	5
December 2010	Impact of KPIs on system design	1(d)	9

6

Performance reports for management

In this chapter

- Reports for performance management.
- Problems dealing with quantitative data.
- Problems dealing with qualitative data.

The output reports (performance reports) produced from a management information system need to be tailored to suit the needs of the users of those reports.

Quantitative information is a key element of these output reports but there are some common mistakes and misconceptions that people make when using numerical data for performance measurement.

Qualitative information should also be a key component of a performance report but is often ignored due to its highly subjective nature.

Reports for performance management

The **purpose** of the report should be considered – does it reflect the mission and objectives?

The **audience** should be considered – the report should be relevant and understandable for the audience.

Considerations when designing a performance report:

The **layout** should be user friendly and avoid information overload.

The **information** must match the purpose. A range of financial and non-financial (quantitative and qualitative) information should be included.

Problems dealing with quantitative data

There are a number of common mistakes and misconceptions that people make when using numerical data for performance management:

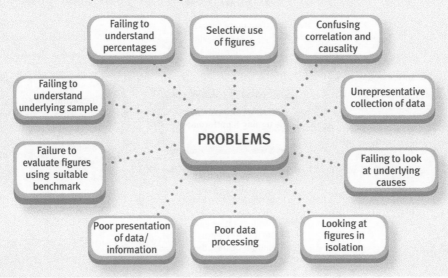

Problems dealing with qualitative data

Definition

Qualitative information is information that cannot normally be expressed in numerical terms.

Qualitative information is often in the form of opinions, e.g. from:

- customers
- employees
- suppliers.

The **subjective** nature of qualitative information makes it more difficult to consider.

Although difficult, qualitative factors should be considered when making a decision.

Exam focus

Exam sitting	Area examined	Question number	Number of marks
Sept/Dec 2017	Evaluation of performance report	1(i)	15
Mar/June 2017	Evaluation of performance report	1(iii)	8
Mar/June 2016	Evaluation of performance report	1(i)	14
December 2014	Qualitative factors	2(c)	7
June 2014	Evaluation of performance report	1(i)	15
December 2013	Wrong signals and dysfunctional behaviour	2(b)	10
June 2013	Evaluation of strategic performance report	1(ii)	8
June 2012	Assessment of performance report	1(i)	12
December 2011	Suitability of branch information given	4(a)	8

7

Human resources aspects of performance management

In this chapter

- Human resources management (HRM).
- Reward scheme for employees and managers.
- Accountability issues arising from performance measurement systems.
- Management styles.

This chapter looks at the link between HRM and performance management and considers the impact of the employee reward system on the behaviour of employees and on the organisation. It also looks at the accountability issues that may arise from performance measurement systems and discusses the need to consider management style when designing a system.

Human resource management (HRM)

Definition

HRM is the strategic and coherent approach to the management of an organisation's most valued assets: the people working there who individually and collectively contribute to the achievement of its objectives for sustainable competitive advantage.

HRM may include recruitment, the development of an appropriate appraisal and reward system and the development of employees.

Today, employees are seen less as an expensive necessity but as a strategic resource that might provide the organisation with competitive advantage.

People are fundamental to an organisation

Strategic significance
- the creation and fulfilment of the strategy relies on the skills, knowledge and creativity of the people.

Operational significance
- successful completion of a task relies on having employees with appropriate skills and abilities to carry out their work.

Rewards scheme for employees and managers

Appropriate **targets** (performance measures) should be set for employees. These should be relevant, achievable, controllable, prioritised and **rewarded**.

Methods:

- Basic pay
- Performance – related pay (PRP):
  - Piecework
  - Individual PRP
  - Group PRP
  - Knowledge contingent pay
  - Commission
  - Profit-related pay
- Benefits
- Share options

Linking reward schemes to performance:

Benefits	Problems
• Motivates staff	• Employees prioritise achievement of reward
• Attracts staff	• Unmotivated if target outside of employee control, difficult to achieve or rewards are inappropriate/ insufficient
• Makes it clear what creates organisational success	• Potential stress
• Focus on continuous improvement	• Potential dysfunctional behaviour
	• How to set targets
	• Cost and time involved establishing an appropriate scheme.

Accountability issues arising from performance measurement systems

Performance measurement systems can distort the processes they are meant to serve. A poorly-designed system can lead to dysfunctional behaviour.

Sending wrong signals can result in inappropriate action.

- Misrepresentation.
- Gaming.
- Misinterpretation.
- Short-termism (mypoia).
- Measure fixation.
- Tunnel vision.
- Sub-optimisation.
- Ossification (lack of flexibility).

A number of actions can be taken to minimise the impact of these imperfections or to avoid them in the first place.

Management styles

Hopwood identified three distinct management styles of performance appraisal. The style needs to be considered when designing an effective performance management system.

- Budget constrained – short-term financial performance is measured using, say, ROCE.
- Profit-conscious – measures of long-term profitability, such as NPV, may be used.
- Non-accounting – non-financial measures, such as customer satisfaction, are used.

Exam focus

Exam sitting	Area examined	Question number	Number of marks
Sept/Dec 2017	Management styles	3(c)	10
Mar/June 2017	Reward scheme assessment	1(v)	12
Mar/June 2016	Reward systems	2(b)	11
June 2015	Management styles	4(c)	10
June 2015	Reward systems	3(c)	9
June 2014	Appraisals	2(c)	8
December 2012	Reward schemes	1(iii)	10
December 2011	Performance appraisal system, Hopwood	4(b) and (c)	12

Financial performance measures in the private sector

In this chapter

- Objectives of a profit-seeking organisation.
- Financial measures of performance.
- Short- and long-term financial performance.

Exam focus

In the exam, you may be required to look at performance measures from a variety of contexts. In this chapter we focus on the principle financial measures used by the private sector.

Objectives of a profit-seeking organisation

Main objective of a business is to maximise shareholder wealth.

- Shareholders are the legal owners of the company.
- They are concerned with the following aspects of financial performance:
  - current earnings
  - future earnings
  - dividend policy
  - relative risk of the investment.

Financial measures of performance

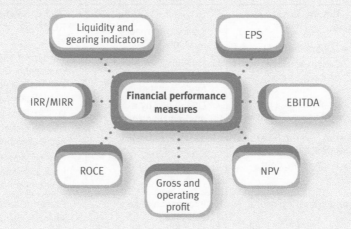

Indicator	Advantages	Disadvantages
ROCE – Return on capital employed $ROCE = \dfrac{\text{Operating profit}}{\text{Capital employed}} \times 100$ If operating profit is not given, use the profit figure closest to it. Capital employed = total assets less current liabilities or total equity plus long-term debt.	• Simple to calculate. • Figures are readily available. • Measure how well a business is using the funds invested in it. • Often used by external analysts/investors.	• Poor correlation between ROCE and shareholder value. • Care must be taken to ensure that like is compared with like e.g. inclusion of intangibles in capital employed. • Can be distorted by accounting policies. • Can be improved by cutting back investment – may lead to short-termism.
Gross and operating profit	• Information readily available. • Managers understand it. • Comparisons between companies easy. • Excludes uncontrollable factors such as tax.	• Profit may be manipulated. • Absolute figures make comparisons difficult. • Poor correlation to shareholder wealth.

Earnings per share (EPS) $$EPS = \frac{\text{PAT} - \text{preference dividends}}{\text{weighted ave. number of ordinary shares in issue}}$$	• Easily understood by shareholders. • Calculation is precisely defined by accounting standards. • Figures are readily available. • Widely used.	• Accounting treatment may cause ratios to be distorted. • Poor correlation between EPS growth and shareholder value.
EBITDA Earnings before interest, tax, depreciation, amortisation and write-offs (such as goodwill).	• Measures underlying performance. • Ignores impact of tax, interest and depreciation. • Easy to calculate. • Easy to understand.	• Ignores changes in working capital. • Poor correlation to shareholder wealth. • Fails to consider the amount of fixed asset replacement needed by the business. • Can easily be manipulated. • Comparisons between organisations difficult due to different accounting policies and calculation of an absolute figure.

NPV		
• Based on DCF analysis. • Looks at present value of cash inflows less present value of outflows of project. • Any project with a positive NPV is viable.	• Strong correlation with shareholder value. • It considers the time value of money. • Risk can be considered. • Cash flows less subject to manipulation and subjective decisions than accounting profits. • Considers all cash flows of a project.	• Difficult to calculate/ understand. • It does not easily allow two projects of very different scales to be compared. • It is based on assumptions about cash flow, the timing and the cost of capital. • Challenging to use for target-setting.
IRR		
• Discount rate when NPV = 0. • Accept project if IRR > firm's cost of capital.	• Provides alternative to NPV when cost of capital of project is uncertain.	• Possible to get multiple rates of return. • More difficult to calculate and to understand than NPV.
MIRR		
• Represents the actual return generated by a project.	• Eliminates the problems associated with IRR. • As for IRR.	• More difficult to calculate and to understand than NPV.

Other profitability ratios

Used alongside main measures such as ROCE.

Asset turnover	$\dfrac{\text{Sales}}{\text{Capital employed}}$
Dividend cover	$\dfrac{\text{PAT}}{\text{Dividends paid during the year}}$
Dividend yield	$\dfrac{\text{Dividend per share}}{\text{Current share price}} \times 100\%$
P/E ratio	$\dfrac{\text{Share price}}{\text{EPS}}$
Earnings yield	$\dfrac{\text{EPS}}{\text{Share price}} \times 100\%$
Return on equity	$\dfrac{\text{Net profit after tax}}{\text{Average shareholder's equity}}$

Liquidity ratios

There is often a trade-off between liquidity and profitability. Liquidity needs to be considered alongside profitability when assessing a company's financial situation.

Current ratio	$\dfrac{\text{Current assets}}{\text{Current liabilities}}$
Acid test (quick ratio)	$\dfrac{\text{Current assets} - \text{inventories}}{\text{Current liabilities}}$
Raw material period	$\dfrac{\text{Average value of raw materials}}{\text{Purchases}} \times 365$
WIP period	$\dfrac{\text{Average value of WIP}}{\text{Cost of sales}} \times 365$
Finished goods period	$\dfrac{\text{Average value of finished}}{\text{Cost of sales}} \times 365$
Receivables period	$\dfrac{\text{Average receivables}}{\text{Sales revenue}} \times 365$
Payables period	$\dfrac{\text{Average payables}}{\text{Purchases}} \times 365$

Risk ratios

These ratios measure the ability of the company to meet its long-term liabilities

Financial gearing	$\dfrac{\text{Long-term debt (LTD)}}{\text{Shareholders' funds}} \times 100\%$
	or
	$\dfrac{\text{LTD}}{\text{LTD + Shareholders' funds}} \times 100\%$
Operating gearing	$\dfrac{\text{Fixed costs}}{\text{Variable costs}}$
Interest cover	$\dfrac{\text{PBIT}}{\text{Interest charges}}$

Short- and long-term financial performance

WAYS TO REDUCE SHORT – TERMISM.

Incorporate both financial and non-financial measures, for example via a balanced scorecard approach.

Switch from a budget – constrained to a profit – conscious or non-accounting style (Hopwood).

Give managers share options to focus their attention on longer-term factors.

Link bonuses to profits over longer timescales than one year.

Ensure that potential investments are assessed on the basis of NPV.

Reduce the degree of decentralisation to ensure stronger central control.

Incorporate value-based management techniques.

Exam focus

Exam sitting	Area examined	Question number	Number of marks
Sept/Dec 2017	ROCE, EBITDA	2(a)	16
Sept/Dec 2016	Evaluation of performance measures, ROCE	1(ii)(iii)	23
June 2014	Fixed and Variable costs	1(ii)	6
June 2013	Evaluation of strategic performance report and metrics	1(ii)	8
December 2012	ROCE	3(b)	7
December 2012	Financial performance evaluation and choice of measures	1(i)(ii)	20
June 2012	Evaluation of performance measures	1(ii)(iii)	24

9

Divisional performance appraisal and transfer pricing

In this chapter

- Problems associated with divisional structures.
- Responsibility accounting.
- Divisional performance measures.
- Value-based management.
- Transfer pricing.

Many modern businesses are split into divisions. You need to be able to discuss the problems that may arise as a result of a divisional structure, the methods that can be used to appraise performance and the use of a value based management approach.

You need to be able to discuss the advantages and disadvantages of transfer pricing systems, the behavioural issues associated with them, and how to design a system. This may require you to generate a simple transfer pricing example to illustrate the issues.

Problems associated with divisional structures

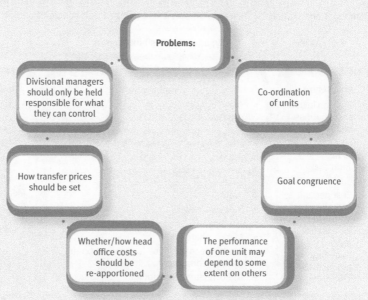

Problems:

- Co-ordination of units

- Goal congruence

- The performance of one unit may depend to some extent on others

- Whether/how head office costs should be re-apportioned

- How transfer prices should be set

- Divisional managers should only be held responsible for what they can control

Responsibility accounting

A manager should only be held accountable and assessed on aspects of performance they control.

```
· · · · · · · · · ·  [ Types of responsibility centre ]  · · · · · · · · · ·
```

Cost centre

- Division incurs costs but has no revenue stream.

Measures:
- Total cost
- Cost variances
- Cost per unit and other cost ratios, NFPIs, for example, related to quality, productivity, efficiency.

Profit centre

- Division has both costs and revenue.
- Manager does not have the authority to alter the level of investment in the division.

Measures:
As cost centre PLUS
- Sales
- Profit
- Sales variances
- Margins
- Market share
- Working capital ratios (depending on the division concerned)
- NFPIs related to customer satisfaction.

Investment centre

- Division has both costs and revenue.
- Manager does have the authority to invest in new assets or dispose of existing ones.

Measures:
As profit centre PLUS
- Return on investment (ROI)
- Residual income (RI)
- Economic value added (EVA).

Divisional performance measures

Measure	Advantages	Disadvantages
Return on investment (ROI) (Controllable operating profit/ controllable capital employed) × 100% Decision: accept project if ROI > cost of capital	• Widely used and accepted. • Enables comparisons. • Can be broken down into secondary ratios.	• May lead to dysfunctional decision making. • Depreciation methods will result in ROI improving with the age of an asset (use annuity depreciation). • Different accounting policies can confuse comparisons. • Excludes intangible assets from capital employed. • Corporate objectives of maximising shareholders' wealth are not achieved by making decisions on the basis of ROI. • May encourage the manipulation of profit and capital employed.

Measure	Advantages	Disadvantages
Residual income (RI) Controllable operating profit X less: imputed interest X RI X • Imputed interest = controllable capital employed x cost of capital. • Decision: accept the project, if the RI is positive.	• Reduces the problems of ROI, i.e. dysfunctional behaviour and holding on to old assets. • Interpreting the result is simple. • Highlights cost of financing a division. • Different cost of capitals can be applied to different divisions based on their risk profiles.	• It does not always result in decisions that are in the best interests of the company (EVA is a superior measure). • Does not take into account the size of the investment or organisation. • Different accounting policies can confuse comparisons. • It is difficult to decide upon an appropriate cost of capital. • May encourage manipulation of profit and capital employed.

Measure	Advantages	Disadvantages
Economic value added (EVA) NOPAT X Adjusted value of capital employed at start of year × WACC (X) EVA X • A similar but superior measure to RI. • Decision: accept the project if the EVA is positive.	• EVA is consistant with NPV and should create real wealth for shareholders. • The adjustments made avoid distortion by accounting policies and should therefore result in goal congruent decisions. • Emphasises cost of financing to division's manager. • Long-term value-adding expenditure can be capitalised, removing any incentive for managers to take a short-term view. • Interpreting the result is simple.	• Requires numerous adjustments to profit and capital employed figures. • Many assumptions made when calculating WACC. • Absolute measure (as is RI) so divisional comparisons difficult. • Based on historical data where as shareholders are interested in future performance.

How to calculate EVA

NOPAT

Controllable operating profit	X
Add:	
accounting depreciation	X
increase in provisions	X
non-cash expenses	X
advertising, r&d, employee training	X
operating lease payments	X
Deduct:	
economic depreciation	(X)
decrease in provisions	(X)
amortisation of advertising, r&d and employee training	(X)
depreciation of operating lease payments	(X)
tax paid including lost tax relief on interest	(X)
= NOPAT	X

Adjusted value of capital employed at the beginning of the year

Main adjustments to capital employed figure are:

- adjustment to reflect replacement cost of non-current assets rather than the book value
- adjustment to reflect economic and not accounting depreciation
- add back value of provisions in period
- add non-cash expenses to retained profit at the end of the year
- increase for expenditure on advertising, r&d and employee training
- add present value of future lease payments.

WACC

- WACC = (proportion of equity x cost of equity) + (proportion of debt x post tax cost of debt).

Value-based management

Definition

Value-based management (VBM) is
an approach to management whereby
the company's strategy, objectives and
processes are aligned to help the company
focus on **key drivers** of shareholder wealth
and hence maximise this value.

Value drivers include revenue, operating
margin, cash tax rate, incremental capital
expenditure, investment in working capital,
cost of capital and growth period.

Measures used in VBM:

* Economic value added (EVA)
* Market value added (MVA)
* Shareholder value analysis

Implementing VBM:

* Develop a strategy to maximise value
* Value drivers indentified and long-term
  and short-term performance targets are
  defined for these drivers
* A plan is developed to achieve these
  targets
* Performance metrics and reward
  systems are created compatible with
  these targets.

VBM evaluation

VBM focuses on value (not profit) making
the organisation more forward looking.
However, it can become an exercise in
valuing everything and changing nothing. In
addition, the MIS will need to be adapted to
take account of new measures.

(Note: the pros and cons of EVA are also
relevant since this is one of the main
measures used).

Transfer pricing

Definition

The transfer price is the price at which goods and services are transferred from one division to another in the same organisation.

Characteristics of a good transfer price:

- Goal congruence

- Fair for divisions

- Autonomy for divisions

- Assists book keeping

- Minimises global tax liability

General rules for setting transfer prices

Perfect competition in market for intermediate product
- Transfer at market price.

Surplus capacity
- Minimum price selling division will accept = marginal cost.
- Maximum price the buying division will pay is the lower of the external purchase price (if available) and the net marginal revenue.

Production constraints
- Minimum price selling division will accept = marginal cost + lost contribution from other product.
- Maximum price the buying division will pay is the lower of the external purchase price (if available) and the net marginal revenue.

Practical methods of transfer pricing

Cost plus

- Producer calculates unit cost.
- May add margin to guarantee profit.
- Use standard cost to avoid passing on inefficiencies and ensure variances reported in division responsible.

Market price based

- Perfect competition for product.
- Division's product must be same as offered by market.
- Adjust market price for costs not incurred on internal transfer.

Issue

- Selling division wants to use total cost to ensure recover fixed overheads.
- Buying division will not want to be charged for fixed costs.

Solutions

- Two part tariff – the selling division transfers each unit at marginal cost and a periodic transfer is made to cover fixed costs.
- Dual pricing – selling and buying divisions record different transfer prices.

International transfer pricing

Important because almost 2/3 world trade takes place within multi-national companies. Issues are:

- taxation
- remittance controls.

Taxation

- Altering the transfer price between divisions in different countries moves profit between countries.
- Anti-avoidance legislation tax authorities can treat the transaction as having taken place at a fair 'arms length' price and revise the profits accordingly.

Remittance controls

- Government of host country in which investment has been made imposes restriction on amount of profit returned to the parent company. This limits parent's ability to pay dividends to shareholders.

- May be done through exchange controls.
- May be avoided by:
  - increasing transfer prices paid by foreign subsidiary
  - lending equivalent of dividend to parent company
  - making payments to parent in other forms, for example management charges.
- Foreign government may try to prevent the above measures.

Exam sitting	Area examined	Question number	Number of marks
Mar/June 2017	Divisional performance measures including the use of net profit and EVA	4	25
Sept/Dec 2016	Transfer pricing	4(b)(c)	17
Mar/June 2016	Divisional performance appraisal	1(ii)-(iv)	24
Sept/Dec 2015	Responsibility centres	3(b)(ii)	4
Sept/Dec 2015	EVA	1(i)	15
June 2015	EVA, ROI and RI, responsibility centres	4	25
June 2014	EVA and VBM	1(iii)(iv)	19
June 2013	Transfer pricing	4	25
December 2012	EVA	3(a)	13
June 2012	EVA	1(ii)	3
June 2011	RI, ROI, EVA, transfer pricing	1(a)(b)	24
December 2010	EVA and VBM	3	20

10

Performance management in not-for-profit organisations

In this chapter

- What is a not-for-profit organisation?
- Problems associated with performance management.
- The use of league tables (benchmarking) and targets in the public sector.

You need to be able to discuss the issues which affect not-for-profit organisations and the implications of these for performance management.

What is a not-for-profit organisation?

Profit is not the main objective.

Performance considers both financial and non-financial issues.

Most do not have external shareholders.

NOT FOR PROFIT

Public sector e.g. healthcare, defence, education, museums.

They do not distribute dividends.

Private sector e.g. charities and sports associations.

Objectives include some social, cultural, philanthropic, welfare or environmental dimension.

Problems associated with performance management

1. Many of the benefits and costs are non-quantifiable. Many orgaisations use cost benefit analysis to quantify these items in financial terms.

4. Impact of politics on performance measurement
- organisations suffer political interference
- long-term objectives sacrificed for short-term political gain.

FOUR KEY PROBLEMS

2. Assessing value for money, especially in public sector organisations receiving a fixed budget for spending from government.

3. Objectives are:
- diverse i.e. different organisations will have different objectives
- multiple – need to prioritise and compromise between the different needs of multiple stakeholders.

Assessing value for money (VFM)

VFM measures whether the organisation has met stakeholders' expectation of best value for the limited funds available.

Assessing value for money can be achieved by:

- analysing economy, efficiency and effectiveness (the 3Es)
- benchmarking
- using performance indicators
- conducting VFM studies or VFM internal audit work.

The 3Es

- Economy – an input measure. Are the resources the cheapest possible for the quality desired?
- Efficiency – is the maximum output being acheived from the resources used?
- Effectiveness – are objectives being met?

Appropriate performance measures should be chosen for each 'E'.

The use of league tables (benchmarking) and targets in the public sector

League tables have become increasingly popular in the public sector in recent years.

They are used to compare one organisation with another by ranking them in order of ability or achievement.

Advantages	Disadvantages
• Stimulates competition and the adoption of best practice.	• Input data may be poor.
	• Outcomes valued by society may be ignored if they are not measurable.
• Monitors and ensures accountability of providers.	• Encourages providers to focus on performance measures rather than the quality of the service.
• Performance is transparent.	• May encourage creative accounting.
	• Differences between providers may make comparisons meaningless.
• League tables should be readily available and can be used by consumers to make choices.	• A low ranking may have a negative impact on public trust and employee morale.
	• A low ranking could lead to a worsening of the future performance.

Benchmarking will be used to rank the organisation in the league table.

A **performance target** represents the level of performance that the organisation aims to achieve for a particular activity. Such targets should be SMART.

Exam sitting	Area examined	Question number	Number of marks
Sept/Dec 2017	NFPIs, VFM	3(a)(b)	15
Mar/June 2016	VFM and league tables	4	25
December 2014	VFM and performance indicators	2(b)	12
December 2013	League tables	4	25
June 2012	Public sector benchmarking	4	17

11

Non-financial performance indicators

In this chapter

- Drawbacks of sole reliance on financial performance measures.
- Non-financial performance indicators.
- Models for evaluating financial and non-financial performance.

Exam focus

In order to fully appraise the performance of an organisation, it is useful to use a range of financial and non-financial performance indicators.

Drawbacks of sole reliance on financial performance measures

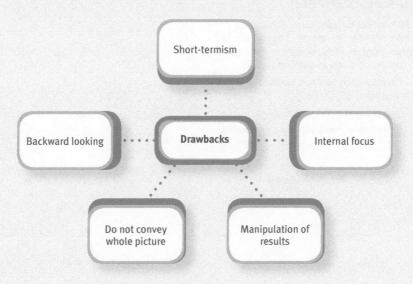

Non-financial performance indicators (NFPIs)

NFPIs reflect the long-term viability and health of the organisation. They should be used alongside FPIs, which are still important in monitoring financial performance.

NFPIs play a key role in a number of areas. For example:

- product and service quality
- brand awareness and company profile.

Models for evaluating financial and non-financial performance

A number of models have been developed to facilitate a broader approach to measuring performance and the identification of a comprehensive range of measures. These look at different perspectives of performance and both financial and non-financial issues.

The balanced scorecard

- Includes financial measures and non-financial measures.
- Includes internal and external information.

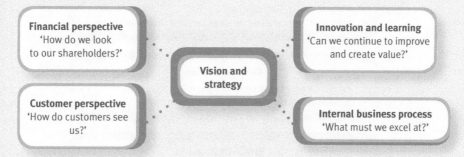

Within each perspective the organisation should identify a series of goals (CSFs) and establish appropriate measures (KPIs) in line with the overall vision and strategy.

Implementing the balanced scorecard

Make the strategy explicit

- Strategy forms the basis of the scorecard.
- May involve strategy mapping.

Choose the measures

- Align measures with strategy.
- Relationships between measures must be clearly understood.

Define and refine

- Put performance measures into place.
- Scorecard becomes the language of the company.

Deal with people

- People and change must be properly managed.
- Rewards aligned to achieve targets.

Advantages of balanced scorecard	Disadvantages of balanced scorecard
• Includes financial measures – these reveal the results of actions taken.	• Difficult to record and process qualitative data.
• Includes non-financial measures – these drive future financial performance.	• Information overload.
• Covers internal and external matters.	• Focuses on strategic level.
• Links achievement of long-term and short-term objectives to achievement of strategy and vision.	• Lack of commitment by senior management.
• Distorting performance harder if multiple measures used.	• Conflict between measures.
• It is flexible and can change over time to reflect changing priorities.	• Poor communication to employees and manager threatens success.
• 'What gets measured gets done' so managers will pay attention to the various aspects of performance that they know they are being appraised on.	• The lack of some key perspectives, for example CSR.
	• The cost involved.

The building block model

Building blocks of performance

Dimensions

Standards

Rewards

Six generic dimensions of performance:

Downstream results:
- Competitiveness
- Financial performance

Upstream determinants:
- Quality of service
- Flexibility
- Resource utilisation
- Innovation

Three main concepts:
- Ownership
- Achievability
- Equity

Motivation achieved through standards that are:
- clear and
- linked to controllable factors.

Advantages of building block model	Disadvantages of building block model
The first five advantages discussed for the balanced scorecard are relevant. In addition: • Tailored for service industry. • It differentiates between downstream results and upstream determinants. • Targets are set in such a way to engage and motivate staff, i.e. due to ownership, achievability and fairness. • Reward system should optimally motivate staff due to it being clear and linked to controllable factors.	The first six disadvantages discussed for the balanced scorecard are relevant. In addition: • It is less suitable for non-service companies. • Difficult to see how building blocks link to strategic objectives.

The performance pyramid (Lynch and Cross)

- Defines the links between objectives and performance measures at different levels in the organisation.
- Designed to ensure that activities of every department, system and business unit support the overall organisational vision.

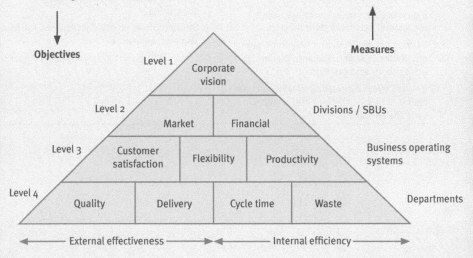

Advantages of performance pyramid	Disadvantages of performance pyramid
The first five advantages discussed for the balanced scorecard are relevant. In addition: • It is hierarchical requiring senior managers to set objectives and relevant performance measures for each level of the organisation. • It is process focused considering how processes combine to achieve organisational goals. Considers the interaction of measures both horizontally and vertically. • Recognises that financial and non-financial measures can support each other.	The first six disadvantages discussed for the balanced scorecard are relevant. In addition: • The model is quite complicated making the time and resources required significant.

Exam sitting	Area examined	Question number	Number of marks
Mar/June 2017	Building block model	1(iv)	6
Sept/Dec 2016	Balanced scorecard	1(i)	8
Sept/Dec 2015	Balanced scorecard	4	25
June 2015	Balanced scorecard	3(a)(b)	16
December 2014	NFPIs in the public sector	2(a)	6
December 2013	Performance pyramid	2(a)	15
June 2013	Balanced scorecard and building block model	1(iii)(iv)(v)	33
December 2011	Performance pyramid	2(b)(c)	18
June 2011	Building block model	3	20
June 2011	Balanced scorecard	2(a)(b)(d)	21

12

Corporate failure

In this chapter

- Why do companies fail?
- Symptoms of failure.
- Corporate failure prediction models.
- Performance improvement strategies.
- The performance management system.
- Long-term survival and the product life-cycle.

So far we have focused on how effective
performance management and measurement
can help an organisation in achieving its
goals. However, not all businesses will
achieve their goals successfully. If left
unchecked these businesses are at risk of
corporate failure.

Why do companies fail?

There are many reasons why companies fail.

Symptoms of failure

There are two main groups of symptoms:

Qualitative
- information in the Chairman's or director's report
- information in the press
- information about environmental or external matters such as changes in the market

Quantitative
- problems with key liquidity, gearing and profitability ratios
- other problems in the published accounts such as a worsening cash position or large increases in intangible fixed assets

Corporate failure prediction models

Altman's Z score

A quantitative model. The Z score is a ratio devised by Robert Altman to describe the financial health of a company, and its likelihood of financial distress.

Z score = $1.2X1 + 1.4X2 + 3.3X3 + 0.6X4 + 1.0X5$

Where:

X1 = working capital/total assets (liquidity)

X2 = retained earnings/total assets (gearing)

X3 = earnings before interest and tax/total assets (productivity of assets)

X4 = market value of equity/total liabilities (equity decline before insolvency)

X5 = sales/total assets (ability of assets to generate revenue)

Score:

- Less than 1.81 – company may be heading towards bankruptcy
- Between 1.81 and 2.99 – company needs further investigation to assess probability of failure
- 3 or above – company financially sound and expected to survive

Advantages:

- Calculation is simple.
- Objective measure.

Disadvantages:

- Score is not a definite predictor.
- More than 50 years old and based on US companies in a specific sector.
- Figures open to manipulation.
- Only a good predictor in the short-term.
- Further analysis needed to fully understand the situation.

Argenti's A score

An example of a qualitative model. Relies on subjective scores to certain questions given by the investigator.

- Defects – management weakness and accounting deficiencies may be included. A score of more than 10/45 is unsatisfactory

- Mistakes – occur as a result of defects and include high gearing, overtrading or failure of a big project. A score of more than 15/45 is unsatisfactory.

- Symptoms of failure – bleak financial indicators, creative accounting, non-financial signs such as high staff turnover and eventual terminal signs.

If the overall score is more than 25, the company has many of the signs preceding failure.

Advantages

- Ability to use non-financial as well as financial measures.

- The ability to use the judgement of the investigator.

These strengths are also **weaknesses**:

- Based on subjective judgement.

- Requires a large amount of financial and non-financial information.

In addition, the model does not consider:

- company specific variables

- general characteristics, such as industry type

- external factors, such as inflation.

Performance improvement strategies

Depends on spotting warning signs and taking quick corrective action.

- Accept that there is a problem and move on to a solution.
- May involve major strategic change.
- Put in controls to prevent further loss.
- Acquiring or developing new businesses (if resources allow) to spread the risk.
- Ensuring different parts of the business are in different stages of the life cycle.
- Learning from mistakes by performing due diligence ahead of an investment.
- Managing major risks such as fluctuations in commodity prices.

The performance management system

The performance management system will need to reflect the performance improvement strategies:

- Establish a link between new strategic goals and CSFs/KPIs.
- Set performance targets at all levels relating to the achievement of strategic objectives.
- Continuous review of actual performance against target.
- Address additional training/ development needs.

Long-term survival and the product life-cycle

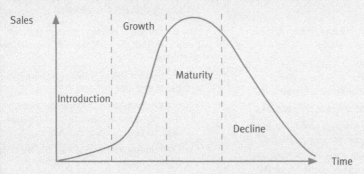

Long-term survival necessitates consideration of life-cycle issues:

Issue 1: there will be different CSFs (and hence KPIs) at different stages in the life-cycle

Issue 2: the stages of the life-cycle have different intrinsic levels of risk which should be understood and responded to.

It will be the scale of the financial resources which the organisation call on over the life of its products which will dictate its survival.

Exam sitting	Area examined	Question number	Number of marks
December 2014	Quantitative models, life-cycle issues, reducing probability of failure	4	20
December 2012	Qualitative models	4	11
December 2010	Corporate failure	5	15
December 2007	Indicators of corporate failure	5(b)	10

13

The role of quality in performance management

In this chapter

- What is quality?
- Quality-related costs.
- Quality practices.
- Lean production.

In today's competitive global business environment, quality is one of the key ways in which a business can differentiate its product or service, improve performance and gain competitive advantage. Quality can form a key part of strategy.

What is quality?

Definition

Quality can be defined in a number of ways:

- Is the product/service free from errors and does it adhere to design specifications?

- Is the product fit for service/use?

- Does the product/service meet customers' needs?

Definition

A **quality management system** is a set of co-ordinated activities to direct and control an organisation in order to continually improve its performance.

Quality-related costs

Monitoring the costs of quality is key to the operation of any quality improvement programme.

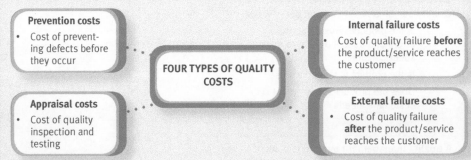

Prevention costs
- Cost of preventing defects before they occur

Appraisal costs
- Cost of quality inspection and testing

FOUR TYPES OF QUALITY COSTS

Internal failure costs
- Cost of quality failure **before** the product/service reaches the customer

External failure costs
- Cost of quality failure **after** the product/service reaches the customer

The organisation's costing system should be capable of identifying and collecting these costs.

KPIs should be developed based on the costs of quality and these can be used as a basis for staff rewards.

Quality practices

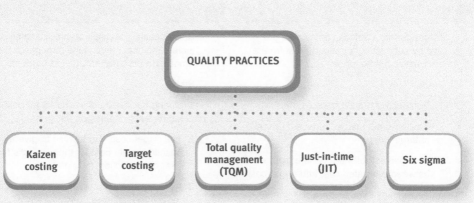

Target costing

Target costing involves setting a target cost by subtracting a desired profit from a competitive market price.

Steps:

1. Competitive market price established.

2. Desired profit margin deducted to arrive at target cost.

3. Cost gap established, i.e. the difference between estimated cost and target cost.

4. Techniques used to close the gap. A value analysis focus should be taken.

Target costing usually occurs at the beginning of a product's life. Kaizen costing uses the principles of target costing but the target cost is revised on a regular basis.

Kaizen costing

Kaizen costing focuses on producing small, incremental cost reductions throughout the production process through the products life.

Steps:

1 During the design phase, a target cost is set for each production function.

2 The target costs are totalled to give a baseline target cost for the product's first year of production.

3 As the process improves, cost reductions reduce the baseline cost.

4 Cost reduction targets are set on a regular basis and variance analysis is carried out.

A traditional costing system is inappropriate in a Kaizen environment.

Total quality management (TQM)

Prevention of errors before they occur

Real participation by all

Features

Management commitment

Continual improvement

Performance measures should be linked to the programme's CSFs.

Just-in-time

Definition

Just-in-time (JIT) is a system whose objective is to produce or procure products or components as they are required rather than for inventory.

Requirements:

- High quality and reliability.
- Elimination of non-value added activities.
- Speed of throughput to match demand.
- Flexibility.
- Lower costs.

Traditional performance measures such as inventory turnover will be replaced with more appropriate measures, such as total head count and productivity.

Six sigma

Aims to reduce the number of faults that go beyond an accepted tolerance level of 3.4 defects per 1 million units produced.

Step 1: **D**efine the process

Step 2: **M**easure existing problems

Step 3: **A**nalyse the process

Step 4: **I**mprove the process

Step 5: **C**ontrol the process

Lean production

Lean production is a philosophy of management based on cutting out waste and unnecessary activities including:

- Over-production
- Inventory
- Waiting
- Defective units
- Motion
- Transportation
- Over-processing

The **five Ss** concept is often associated with lean principles and has the aim of creating a workplace which is in order.

Five Ss	Explanation
Structurise	Introduce order where possible.
Systemise	Arrange and identify items for ease of use and systematic approach.
Sanitise	Be tidy, avoid clutter.
Standardise	Be consistent in approach taken.
Self-discipline	Do above daily.

Lean MIS

A quality MIS should be functional, usable, reliable and easy to maintain.

A lean approach would identify and eliminate waste in the MIS. For example, the MIS should:

- only produce a report that adds value.

- only produce a report for the people who need it.

- be capable of real time processing.

- produce information that is accurate, clear and retrieved easily.

- eliminate waste such as data duplication.

- be flexible to adapt to changing needs.

- be continually improved.

Exam focus

Exam sitting	Area examined	Question number	Number of marks
Sept/Dec 2017	Target costing, TQM, quality costs	1(iii)(iv)	25
Mar/ June 2017	Target costing, Kaizen costing	2	25
Sept/Dec 2016	Quality costs, TQM, lean systems	1(iv)(v)	15
Sept/Dec 2015	Lean, JIT, Kaizen, quality costs	1(iii)(iv)	25
Sept/Dec 2015	DMAIC	3(a)	15
December 2014	JIT	1(iv)	7
December 2013	Lean management and accountability	3(b)(c)	13
June 2012	Six Sigma	3	17
December 2011	Quality costs, Kaizen and JIT	5	20

14

Environmental management accounting

In this chapter

- Drawbacks of traditional management accounting.
- What is EMA?
- EMA techniques.

Exam focus

Organisations are becoming increasingly aware of the environmental implications of their actions.

Drawbacks of traditional management accounting

Managers need to be able to identify the environmental costs that exist in order to be able to measure existing performance and to monitor the effectiveness of any environmental-related activities undertaken.

Traditional management accounting systems are unable to adequately deal with environmental costs:

Type of environmental cost	Problem
Conventional costs, e.g. energy costs.	Not prioritised since often hidden in overheads.
Contingent costs, e.g. decommissioning costs.	Often ignored due to short-term focus.
Relationship costs, e.g. cost of producing environmental information for reporting.	Ignored by managers who may be unaware of their existence.
Reputational cost, i.e. the cost of failing to address environmental issues.	Ignored by managers who are unaware of the risk of incurring them.

What is EMA?

1. It is concerned with the accounting information needs of managers; identifying and estimating the costs of environment-related activities and seeking to control these costs.

2. It assesses the likelihood and impact of environmental risks.

3. It considers the non-financial environmental cost and benefit of any decisions made as well as the financial cost and benefit.

4. It includes environmental-related KPIs as part of routine performance monitoring.

5. It benchmarks activities against environmental best practice.

EMA techniques

ABC	• Removes environment-driven costs from overheads and traces them to products or services. • Should result in the identification of cost drivers and better control of costs.
Lifecycle costing	• Considers the costs and revenues of a product over its whole life rather than one accounting period. • In order to reduce lifecycle costs may use techniques such as TQM.
Flow cost accounting	• Looks at material flows and material losses at various stages of production. • Aims to reduce the quantities of material. • Related to input output analysis which focuses on waste in a process.

Exam sitting	Area examined	Question number	Number of marks
Sept/Dec 2016	EMA and lifecycle	3(b)(c)	17
December 2014	EMA	3	25
June 2011	EMA	5	20
December 2010	Environmental performance	4	20

Index

Symbols

A

B

C

KAPLAN PUBLISHING